NATIONAL GEOGRAPHIC | **GLOBAL ISSUES**

HABITAT
PRESERVATION

Andrew J. Milson, Ph.D.
Content Consultant
University of Texas at Arlington

Acknowledgments

Grateful acknowledgment is given to the authors, artists, photographers, museums, publishers, and agents for permission to reprint copyrighted material. Every effort has been made to secure the appropriate permission. If any omissions have been made or if corrections are required, please contact the Publisher.

Instructional Consultant: Christopher Johnson, Evanston, Illinois

Teacher Reviewer: Julie Mitchell, Lake Forest Middle School, Cleveland, Tennessee

Photographic Credits

Front Cover, Inside Front Cover, Title Page
©Chris Newbert/Minden Pictures. **4** (bg) ©imago stock&people/Newscom. **6** (bg) ©Jacques Jangoux/ Photo Researchers/Getty Images. **7** (bl) ©Carl Purcell/ Carl & Ann Purcell/Corbis. **8** (bg) Mapping Specialists. **10** (bg) ©Stephen Morrison/EPA/Newscom. **11** (tl) ©Ralph Paprzycki/Alamy. **12** (tr) Mapping Specialists. **13** (bg) ©Andrew Holbrooke/Corbis. **14** (bg) ©Michael Nichols/National Geographic Stock. **15** (tl) ©Michael Nichols/National Geographic Stock. **16** (bg) ©David Doubilet/National Geographic Stock. **18** (tr) ©Michael Patrick O'Neill/Woodfall Wild Images/Photoshot. **19** (bg) ©imagebroker. net/SuperStock. **20** (bg) ©Matthew Oldfield/Photo Researchers, Inc. **22** (bg) ©Tom Brakefield/Corbis. **23** (tl) ©Beverly Joubert/National Geographic Stock. **24** (bg) ©Beverly Joubert/National Geographic Stock. **27** (t) ©AP Photo/John David Mercer. **28** (tr) ©LeoFFreitas/Flickr/Getty Images. **30** (tr) ©imago stock&people/Newscom. (br) ©David Doubilet/ National Geographic Stock. **31** (bg) ©PhotoDisc/Getty Images. (tr) ©Universal Images Group/SuperStock. (br) ©Jim Zuckerman/Corbis. (bl) ©Peter Solness/ Lonely Planet Images/Getty Images.

MetaMetrics® and the MetaMetrics logo and tagline are trademarks of MetaMetrics, Inc., and are registered in the United States and abroad. The trademarks and names of other companies and products mentioned herein are the property of their respective owners. Copyright © 2010 MetaMetrics, Inc. All rights reserved.

For permission to use material from this text or product, submit all requests online at www.cengage.com/permissions.

Further permissions questions can be emailed to permissionrequest@cengage.com.

Visit National Geographic Learning online at www.NGSP.com.

Visit our corporate website at www.cengage.com.

Printed in the USA.

RR Donnelley, Menasha, WI

ISBN: 978-07362-97783

14 15 16 17 18 19 20 21 22 23

11 10 9 8 7 6 5 4 3

SAVIN

Habitat

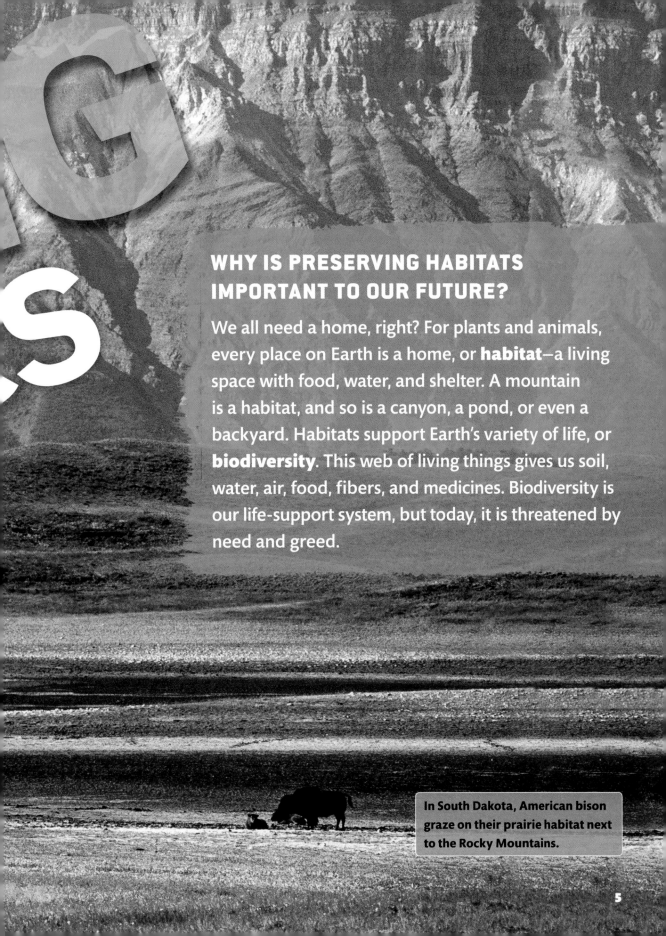

WHY IS PRESERVING HABITATS IMPORTANT TO OUR FUTURE?

We all need a home, right? For plants and animals, every place on Earth is a home, or **habitat**—a living space with food, water, and shelter. A mountain is a habitat, and so is a canyon, a pond, or even a backyard. Habitats support Earth's variety of life, or **biodiversity**. This web of living things gives us soil, water, air, food, fibers, and medicines. Biodiversity is our life-support system, but today, it is threatened by need and greed.

In South Dakota, American bison graze on their prairie habitat next to the Rocky Mountains.

THREATS CLOSE TO HOME

In 2011, Earth's human population topped 7 billion. These billions increased the demand for land, water, and other resources. The human population is damaging many habitats and the **species**, or kinds of living things, that need them. When habitats disappear, species die and biodiversity suffers.

Agriculture is one major cause of habitat loss. Most of the world's poorest 1 billion people are farmers. They expand their farms into forests as they need more land and energy. The removal of trees in a forest to use the land for farming or other uses is called **deforestation**. Fertilizers and **pesticides**, or chemicals that kill insects and other pests, cause further damage.

Urban sprawl—the spread of cities into surrounding land— also eats up pastures, wetlands, and forests. Each day in the United States, 6,000 acres of land are lost to housing, factories, and malls. That equals 4,500 football fields!

This method of deforestation in Brazil is called slash-and-burn. Farmers commonly use this method to get more land for planting.

GLOBAL WORRIES

Wealthy and developing countries use 5 to 10 times more resources than the poorest countries. The actions of the richer consumers affect the whole planet. Wealthy countries burn the most fossil fuels, which warm the atmosphere. They consume most of the world's lands, forests, minerals, and fisheries. They also churn out most of the world's garbage, factory wastes, and other pollutants. This **overconsumption** uses resources faster than nature can replace them.

In the last 30 years, people have used one-third of Earth's resources. The result? Habitats are disappearing too fast for species to adjust. If this population growth and consumption continue, we will use up these resources. The United Nations (UN) estimates that every day, 150–200 species become **extinct**, or vanish forever. According to the UN, the world is now facing rapid extinction of the largest number of species since 65 million years ago, when the dinosaurs disappeared.

Conservation is the work of saving habitats and living things. Most conservation fighters turn out to be ordinary people. On the following pages you will read about problems in Kenya and Australia. In these countries, ordinary people came together to solve them.

In the Florida Everglades, habitat destruction has reduced the marsh area to half its former size. This was caused by agriculture, urban sprawl, runoff pollution, and loss of water resources.

Explore the Issue

1. **Identify Problems** What are some major causes of habitat destruction?

2. **Analyze Cause and Effect** How do booming populations and overconsumption affect habitats and biodiversity?

Habitats in

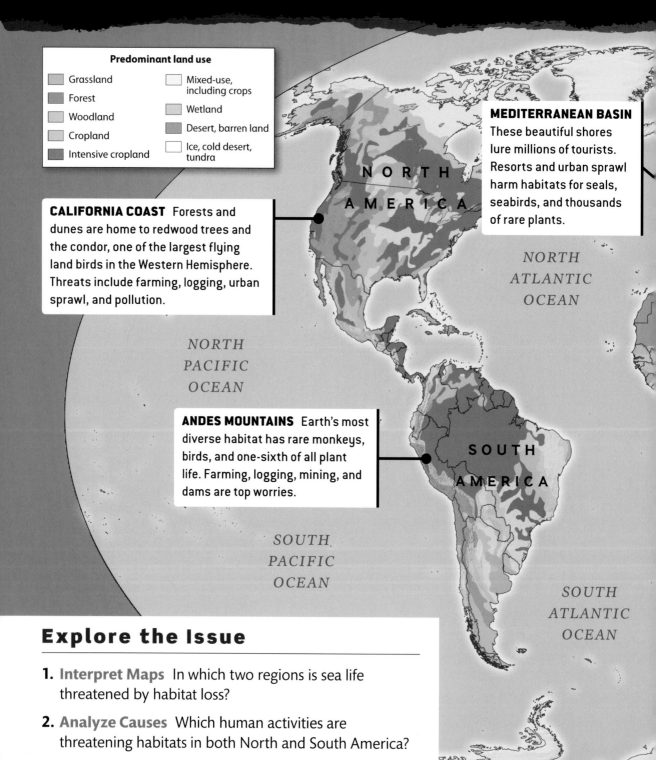

Predominant land use

- Grassland
- Forest
- Woodland
- Cropland
- Intensive cropland
- Mixed-use, including crops
- Wetland
- Desert, barren land
- Ice, cold desert, tundra

MEDITERRANEAN BASIN These beautiful shores lure millions of tourists. Resorts and urban sprawl harm habitats for seals, seabirds, and thousands of rare plants.

CALIFORNIA COAST Forests and dunes are home to redwood trees and the condor, one of the largest flying land birds in the Western Hemisphere. Threats include farming, logging, urban sprawl, and pollution.

ANDES MOUNTAINS Earth's most diverse habitat has rare monkeys, birds, and one-sixth of all plant life. Farming, logging, mining, and dams are top worries.

NORTH AMERICA

SOUTH AMERICA

NORTH PACIFIC OCEAN

SOUTH PACIFIC OCEAN

NORTH ATLANTIC OCEAN

SOUTH ATLANTIC OCEAN

Explore the Issue

1. **Interpret Maps** In which two regions is sea life threatened by habitat loss?

2. **Analyze Causes** Which human activities are threatening habitats in both North and South America?

Danger

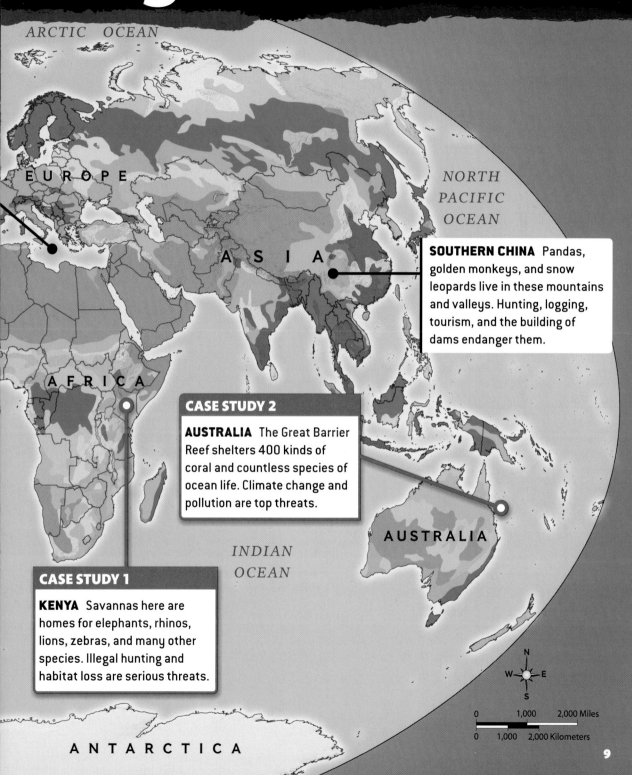

Study the map below to learn about threatened habitats, many with species found nowhere else.

ARCTIC OCEAN

EUROPE

ASIA

NORTH PACIFIC OCEAN

AFRICA

SOUTHERN CHINA Pandas, golden monkeys, and snow leopards live in these mountains and valleys. Hunting, logging, tourism, and the building of dams endanger them.

CASE STUDY 2

AUSTRALIA The Great Barrier Reef shelters 400 kinds of coral and countless species of ocean life. Climate change and pollution are top threats.

AUSTRALIA

INDIAN OCEAN

CASE STUDY 1

KENYA Savannas here are homes for elephants, rhinos, lions, zebras, and many other species. Illegal hunting and habitat loss are serious threats.

N
W — E
S

| 0 | 1,000 | 2,000 Miles |
| 0 | 1,000 | 2,000 Kilometers |

ANTARCTICA

Kenya's ELEPHANT EMERGENCY

An orphaned baby elephant needs love just as much as it needs milk to survive.

IN THE NURSERY

At midday at a water hole near Nairobi, Kenya, a half dozen baby elephants are playing in the mud. These little elephants are here because they have been saved by Dame Daphne Sheldrick's orphanage, part of the David Sheldrick Wildlife Trust. One starving baby, just three days old, was pulled from an open manhole. Another was found speared in the head after hunters killed her mother.

This family of elephants is protected in a national park in Kenya.

Raising battered orphans such as these takes "tender loving care. TLC—and a lot of it," says Sheldrick. Gentle keepers feed the babies every three hours around the clock. They walk with them in the bush and sleep with them at night. Without this constant flow of motherly love, the orphans wouldn't survive.

Yet their survival couldn't be more urgent. In just 30 years, Kenya's elephant population has plunged from 130,000 to 35,000. Today, every life counts.

INTO THE WILD

Orphan elephants depend on milk and constant care until they're two years old. If they survive, they graduate to Tsavo National Park, home to 12,570 wild elephants. Over the next ten years, the orphans grow into adults on Tsavo's **savannas**, grasslands with scattered trees. There, they slowly leave their keepers and join an elephant family in the wild.

Once they're grown, these babies will weigh up to 15,000 pounds—almost as much as four cars! For 16 hours a day, they will forage for huge amounts of food: between 220 and 440 pounds of grass, leaves, and tree bark, polished off with 30 to 50 gallons of water. They will roam up to 1,000 square miles to find food and water—enough habitat to cover Rhode Island.

Tsavo is the biggest of Kenya's 55 reserves. It has 8 times the range needed for elephants. Elephants on smaller reserves must migrate more to find food. Larger preserves provide more of the habitat that elephants need to thrive.

PEOPLE VS. ELEPHANTS

Today, people are both the elephants' best friends and their worst enemies. Kenya's $1 billion tourism business depends on its wildlife, and many groups work hard to protect the animals. At the same time, a booming population of 43 million people is overrunning wild habitats.

About 20 million Kenyans are poor farmers who survive on small plots of land. Their settlements sprawl into unprotected habitats used by 70 percent of Kenya's wild animals. Their villages also block elephant migration routes to seasonal grazing lands.

Naturally, clashes occur. Elephants searching for food sometimes raid farmers' fields of wheat and corn. Occasionally, they attack people. Over the last ten years, one area south of Nairobi recorded 4,500 incidents of damage by elephants. Frustrated villagers in these areas destroy trees to wipe out the elephants' food supply. Although it's illegal to harm elephants, some farmers kill them anyway. In the end, habitats are destroyed and species are lost, a tragedy for wildlife and people.

ELEPHANT RANGE IN KENYA 1979–2007

0   50   100 Miles

0   50 100 Kilometers

Lake Turkana

South Turkana National Reserve

Marsabit National Reserve

KENYA

Samburu National Reserve

Kora N.P.

Tana R.

Lake Victoria

Nairobi
Nairobi N.P.

Masai Mara National Reserve

Amboseli N.P.

Tsavo East National Park

Galana R.

Tsavo West N.P.

INDIAN OCEAN

☐ 1979 Elephant range
■ 2007 Elephant range
— Protected area

Source: *National Geographic Magazine*, September 2011, p. 53

The elephants' habitat is less than half of its size 30 years ago.

KILLED FOR IVORY

A worse threat comes from illegal hunters called **poachers**. During the 1980s, poachers killed more than 80 percent of Kenya's elephants for their ivory tusks, worth fortunes on world markets. In 1989, Kenya outlawed the sale of ivory, saving the 16,000 elephants that remained. Since that time, elephant numbers have rebounded to 35,000.

Today, however, poaching has spiked again. Some wealthy people in developed countries buy ivory trinkets to show off their status. One pound of ivory costs $700 or more. A carved human figure sells for nearly $40,000. Killing elephants can mean easy money. Most poachers come from outside Kenya, and many are professional criminals. They invade reserves in search of the biggest tusks. With automatic rifles, they kill the oldest members of a family, leaving young elephants to die.

To discourage poachers, Kenyan government workers are burning 20 tons of elephant tusks they captured from poachers so they cannot be sold on the world market.

The younger orphan elephants crawl and play on top of the older orphans in their safe habitat at the Sheldrick Trust. These elephants are the hope for future herds.

Local children meet baby elephants at the Tsavo National Park.

FORMING NEW FAMILIES

Poachers, poverty, and skyrocketing population all threaten Kenya's elephants. In response, the Kenya Wildlife Service has hired 500 more rangers to keep poachers away. Settlements have created passages called "corridors" to open migration routes through village areas. The Sheldrick nursery raises orphaned elephants in a normal family. So far, the nursery has saved about 100 orphans and returned them to the wild.

Elephants live in small, close-knit families of about ten female relatives and friends. They are deeply attached because they feel empathy, the ability to experience another's emotions. Family members care for baby elephants. They help loved ones in trouble. When a family member dies, they mourn. Orphaned elephants suffer heartbreak when they lose their mothers. Without the chance to heal, they can grow up angry and dangerous. The orphanage prevents this.

TURNING FOES INTO FRIENDS

The Sheldrick Trust uses many other tactics to rescue elephants. A vital one is winning support from Kenya's farmers. Most children living in poverty have little understanding of habitats and conservation. So the Trust pays for films, wildlife clubs, conservation projects, and bus trips into Tsavo National Park. For thousands of children who have never valued Kenya's wildlife, these experiences can be life-changing.

The elephant keepers—widely admired in Kenya—broadcast radio shows to their tribes. The keepers teach respect for elephants. They explain how killing wildlife, helping poachers, and destroying habitats endangers everyone's future. They also suggest ways to protect crops and urge farmers to help save orphans. These efforts are showing results. A number of villages now care for orphans until keepers arrive, thus saving elephants.

Explore the Issue

1. **Identify Problems** What are the major threats to Kenya's elephants?

2. **Analyze Cause and Effect** How does the Sheldrick Trust help Kenya's elephants?

Trouble on Australia's
GREAT BARRIER REEF

The Great Barrier Reef has at least ten times more coral species than the entire Atlantic Ocean. The survival of this habitat is in grave danger.

CORAL CRISIS

Late in 2000, Australian filmmaker Sally Ingleton discovered trouble on the Great Barrier Reef, which lies off Australia's northeast coast. Mud was flowing from the land and clouding the blue ocean waters. The mud was killing beautiful coral reefs. The reefs are habitat for thousands of species of fish and other ocean life.

Upset by the situation, Ingleton got to work. For the next year she wrote and directed *Muddy Waters*, a documentary film about how the mud was killing the reefs. She wanted people to know about the problem and take action to solve it.

The Great Barrier Reef is a system of 2,900 connected reefs and is about 1,400 miles long, bigger than Italy. This great reef is Earth's largest living organism. An organism is a living body. Though solid underneath, its living surface is powered by the sun. Reefs are built slowly by **coral polyps**, animals that can be as small as pinheads that create hard skeletons around their bodies. Coral polyps get 90 percent of their food from tiny plants called algae that live inside their shells. Like most plants, the algae convert sunlight into food that supports the living coral. Some tiny corals grow up to 6 inches a year. Together, over long periods of time, the corals construct massive reefs.

A HEALTHY HABITAT

The Great Barrier Reef thrives beside tropical Queensland, a large state in northeastern Australia. Here, offshore waters of the Coral Sea are clear, warm, and shallow, ideal conditions for around 400 species of coral. Hard corals, the builders of the reef, look like plates, antlers, and trees. Soft corals in a rainbow of colors resemble whips and fans.

Nooks and crannies in the reef form habitats for countless species. Nearly 2,000 known fish species live there, from tiny clownfish to whale sharks the size of cars. The fish mingle with sea snakes, giant clams, turtles, and other species.

A healthy reef needs healthy habitats on land and along the coasts. The wettest parts of Queensland get up to 14 feet of rain a year. In the past, forests retained most of the soil during heavy rains and floods. Seaside **wetlands**—low-lying lands soaked with water—filtered out pollutants. These natural systems kept reef waters clean and clear.

CATTLE AND SUGARCANE

When people settled Queensland 180 years ago, they began to change its habitat. Cattle ranchers cleared forests to open pastures. To improve their profits, they bought cattle that graze all year long, even in dry weather.

The results have harmed the reef. Millions of cattle strip the pastures and eat the grass along riverbanks. When heavy rains blow in, the rivers flood and wash millions of tons of topsoil out to sea. This soil is deposited and settles to the bottom of the ocean. This soil is called **sediment**.

Destructive fishing practices destroyed this coral reef.

About 6,000 sugarcane farmers also live on the Queensland coast. The roots of sugarcane rot if they stand in watery soil. To protect the sugarcane, farmers cleared more than half of the wetlands and built drains to carry away the water. Today, they use fertilizers to boost their harvests, and pesticides to kill insects and other pests. These chemicals pollute sediment. The wetlands, along with trees called mangroves, once filtered chemicals out of the water. Now the drains sweep water, sediment, and chemicals onto the reefs.

A HEAVY PRICE

Over the last 150 years, the amount of sediment hitting the reef has increased four to eight times. This runoff pollutes hundreds of reefs near shore. Some of these reefs have lost half of their coral.

Sediment and chemicals harm the reef in many ways. Clouds of sediment block the sunlight that coral needs to make food. Then chemicals carried in sediment cause even more damage. Pesticides, even tiny amounts, destroy young, developing corals. Without new corals, the reefs cannot rebuild.

Fertilizers injure growing corals, too, but they also feed free-living algae. These fast-growing algae smother the coral. They also attract predators such as starfish. Just one starfish can destroy about 20 feet of coral in a year.

The white around the edges of this beach in Queensland shows the pollution from fertilizers, pesticides, and runoff. Such pollution threatens the coral reef.

To start to grow more coral, these divers are attaching a bit of coral to a Biorock® structure, a cement-like substance made from minerals through which low voltage electricity flows. The coral will start to grow around the structure after divers give it a jolt of electricity.

RESCUING THE REEF

In 2002, the film *Muddy Waters* stirred up strong debates. Could science prove that runoff of mud hurt the reef? Would reducing use of chemicals hurt farmers' income?

In 2003, the national and Queensland governments announced a $40 million Reef Water Quality Protection Plan. The plan set up partnerships among industry, researchers, conservationists, and communities. It funded research and updated farming methods.

Australians got to work. Reef Guardian Farmers improved their soil and built wetlands to filter runoff. After the harvest, they left plant material behind to protect the soil from heavy rains. Ranchers began to rest their pastures and stream banks by changing where the cattle grazed. More than 60,000 students in 230 Queensland schools also became Reef Guardians. They restored habitats and set up recycling programs. One school in the town of Cairns planted 10,000 trees along Sawpit Gulley to keep topsoil in place.

THE FIGHT GOES ON

Late in 2011, the government reported that one-third of sugarcane farmers had improved their soil and cut back on fertilizers. About half of all cattle ranchers also repaired their land. This was good news but not good enough.

Every year, 14 million tons of sediment still hit the reef, enough to fill 100,000 dump trucks. Climate change promises more severe rains. Huge, dirty floods in 2011 sent pollution into 11 percent of reef waters. Scientists note that healthy reefs can handle major disasters, but heavy pollution injures the coral.

Australians know that these efforts are vital. Only nature can build a marvel such as the Great Barrier Reef.

Explore the Issue

1. **Identify Problems** What human activities on land threaten the Great Barrier Reef?

2. **Identify Solutions** What are different groups of Australians doing to try to help save the reefs?

Saving Big Cats

Lion families in Kenya face extinction if their habitats are not saved. Healthy lionesses usually have litters of two to four cubs every two years.

GOING, GOING . . .

Think about these cold, hard facts. In 1960, 450,000 lions roamed the savannas of Africa; today, only 20,000 are left. In just 50 years, more than 90 percent of Africa's lions have been lost. Most of them died because of habitat destruction, poaching, sport hunting, and conflicts with people.

Beverly and Dereck Joubert film wildlife in Africa.

These statistics alarmed conservationists and filmmakers Beverly and Dereck Joubert (joo-BEHR), National Geographic Explorers-in-Residence. For nearly 30 years, the Jouberts have filmed wildlife in Africa. Each of their 22 films delivers a strong conservation message.

As the Jouberts learned, other big cats are also living on the edge of extinction. Wild leopards have dwindled from 750,000 to 50,000. Cheetahs are down from 45,000 to 12,000. The case of tigers is the most shocking of all: only 3,000 still remain in the wild.

"We are seeing the effects of 7 billion people on the planet," Dereck says. "At present rates, we will lose the big cats in 10 to 15 years."

TIME FOR ACTION

To the Jouberts, these numbers signaled a looming disaster. Habitats need predators, such as lions, because they control populations of prey, which are animals the predators eat. Otherwise, too many prey animals strip away plants until the animals die from sickness and starvation. Then habitats crash along with communities that need them.

"We no longer have the luxury of time when it comes to big cats," says Dereck. "They are in such a downward spiral that if we hesitate now, we will be responsible for extinctions across the globe. If there was ever a time to take action, it is now." Therefore, in 2009, the Jouberts teamed with National Geographic to organize a bold **initiative**, or plan of action.

At work, the Jouberts film and photograph a leopard in its habitat.

B·346 ACY

"We no longer have the luxury of time when it comes to big cats." —Dereck Joubert

ROARING BACK

The Jouberts and National Geographic took action to create the Big Cats Initiative (BCI), an emergency fund. It supports fast-action projects to stop the decline of African lions by 2015 and then build numbers to healthy levels by 2020. So far, BCI has sponsored 21 projects in 13 countries. To help fund the BCI, the Jouberts filmed a documentary and appeared on television in the United States. They seek money from all over the world to save the big cats.

The Jouberts face huge challenges. Protecting habitats takes millions of dollars, land for lions, and a global army of supporters. Through the Big Cats Initiative, the Jouberts have hope. Big cats multiply quickly if they are left in peace, and BCI's projects in Africa indicate that could happen.

Another important task for the Jouberts is to try to change the attitudes of people who live near lions. Lions need a huge habitat for hunting and having families. As the African human population grows, agricultural land is taken from the lions' habitat. Hungry lions come looking for prey on farms, part of their previous habitat. Villagers kill lions to protect themselves and their livestock.

BCI tests many ideas with local people. In Tanzania, project leaders show popular films explaining the benefits of lions and ways to coexist. Elsewhere, "living walls" strengthen wildlife pens with chain-link fences and fast-growing trees to better protect cattle from lions. In return, people leave the lions alone.

The plan is showing results in Kenya, where herdsmen are repaid if lions kill their cattle. In a hopeful sign, fewer lions are being lost.

Growing human populations remain a threat, but Dereck Joubert has begun to see promise. "It really depends on what those 7 billion people do. . . . We can build a real army of people fighting for conservation," he says.

Explore the Issue

1. **Analyze Cause and Effect** What human activities have affected the big cats? What is the effect of those activities?

2. **Identify Problems and Solutions** How has the Big Cats Initiative helped preserve habitats?

What Can I DO?

Restore a Habitat
—and document your efforts

You can inspire people to do their part in protecting and preserving habitats. One way is to shine a light on a problem they might not know about. You don't have to be a famous filmmaker to create an informative, engaging documentary. Showing how ordinary people can help encourages others to join in.

IDENTIFY

- Invite an expert from a local nature center, zoo, or botanical park to speak to your class. Learn about ways this organization protects and preserves habitats.

- Ask the expert about biodiversity in your area and habitats that are threatened.

- Find out how your group can help. Ask the expert to identify a center or an organization that could use your help for a day.

ORGANIZE

- Plan a class field trip to your identified location. Discuss with the organization what work you will be performing and what you will need to bring.

- Before arriving, decide how you will document your class's efforts and work for the day.

- Collect notebooks, cameras, and video recorders to use while volunteering.

Students in Alabama plant dune grasses to help restore the coastal habitat.

DOCUMENT

- Interview people who work at the location. In addition, interview fellow students as you work on your volunteer project.

- Take photos of the habitat. Record details about animals and birds, plants, water sources, and current threats.

- Create a multimedia documentary about the location and the work the class performed. Or, create a poster of a series of 10–12 photos with detailed captions.

SHARE

- Show your documentary to people at the location where you volunteered. Offer to have a "live showing" on a particular day. Invite students' families to participate.

- Present your documentary to other classes and/or other grades at your school.

- Offer to write a short article for the school paper about your efforts.

Research & WRITE
Argumentative

Write an Argumentative Article

The Amazon rain forest is one of the largest and most diverse habitats on Earth. Today, deforestation seriously threatens its future and ours. Write an article about the dangers to the Amazon rain forest and what individuals should do to save it. Focus on a specific solution that ordinary people can work toward to help protect this rain forest.

RESEARCH

Use the Internet, books, and articles to research and answer these questions:

- What dangers is the Amazon rain forest facing? What are different viewpoints about its use?
- What agricultural, consumer, and business practices threaten its future? What can or should be done about those practices?
- What is your own viewpoint and possible solution after your research?

Your research is the backbone of your argument. Be sure to take notes and record your sources. Find statistics or quotations to support your viewpoint.

DRAFT

Review your notes and then write a first draft.

- The first paragraph, or introduction, should hook the reader's attention and present the problem. State your argument. Explain what you think should be done, and use evidence to support your claim.
- In the second paragraph, or body, identify the threats to the rain forest that your argument addresses. Use statistics or quotations from your notes, and explain how your ideas will help.
- In the third paragraph, or conclusion, write a final statement arguing for choices that you want people to make to protect the rain forest. Emphasize the importance of your argument.

REVISE & EDIT

Read your first draft to make sure it presents a strong case for choices that protect the rain forest.

- Does your introduction clearly state your claim? Do you introduce your argument and support your claim with clear reasons and relevant evidence?
- Does the body clearly explain activities that harm the rain forest and show how your ideas for improvement will help the situation?
- In your conclusion, have you persuaded readers to make specific changes to help preserve the rain forest?

Revise your article to make sure it covers all the bases. Then proofread your paper for errors in spelling and punctuation. Are names spelled correctly and are quotations accurate? Be sure your argument presents evidence logically and links problems to solutions.

PUBLISH & PRESENT

Now you are ready to publish and present your argument. Add any images or graphs, and then print out or write a clean copy by hand. Post your article in the classroom and discuss your ideas with classmates.

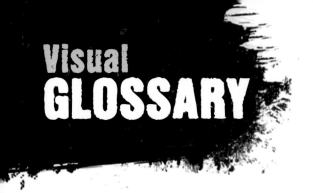

Visual GLOSSARY

habitat

species

biodiversity *n.*, the variety of living things on Earth

conservation *n.*, the work of preserving habitats and living things

coral polyp *n.*, a pinhead-sized animal that builds a hard skeleton and joins with other coral polyps to form coral reefs

deforestation *n.*, the removal of trees in a forest to convert the land to farming or other uses

extinct *adj.*, describing a species that no longer exists

habitat *n.*, the natural home of a living thing, providing food, water, and shelter

initiative *n.*, a plan of action

overconsumption *n.*, the use of natural resources faster than nature can replace them

pesticide *n.*, a chemical that destroys insects or other pests that harm plants and animals

poacher *n.*, a person who hunts illegally

savanna *n.*, a grassland with scattered trees

sediment *n.*, soil carried by water or wind and deposited on land or in a body of water

species *n.*, kinds of living things with similar features that can interbreed

urban sprawl *n.*, the spread of cities into surrounding land

wetland *n.*, a marshy or swampy land area soaked with water

coral polyp

savanna

deforestation

INDEX

SKILLS